SandCastle™

Baby Mammals

It's a Baby

Beaver!

Kelly Doudna

Consulting Editor, Diane Craig, M.A./Reading Specialist

ABDO
Publishing Company

Published by ABDO Publishing Company, 8000 West 78th Street, Edina, Minnesota 55439.

Copyright © 2008 by Abdo Consulting Group, Inc. International copyrights reserved in all countries.

Printed in the United States.

Editor: Pam Price
Content Developer: Nancy Tuminelly
Cover and Interior Design and Production: Mighty Media
Photo Credits: AbleStock, Juniors Bildarchiv, Peter Arnold Inc. (Alan & Sandy Carey, D. Hoell, Chlaus Lotscher, Lynda Richardson, H. Schulz)

Library of Congress Cataloging-in-Publication Data

Doudna, Kelly, 1963-
  It's a baby beaver! / Kelly Doudna.
     p. cm. -- (Baby mammals)
  ISBN 978-1-60453-022-3
1. Beavers--Juvenile literature. 2. Beavers--Infancy--Juvenile literature. I. Title.

QL737.R632D68 2008
599.37'139--dc22

                    2007033739

SandCastle™ Level: Fluent

SandCastle™ books are created by a team of professional educators, reading specialists, and content developers around five essential components—phonemic awareness, phonics, vocabulary, text comprehension, and fluency—to assist young readers as they develop reading skills and strategies and increase their general knowledge. All books are written, reviewed, and leveled for guided reading, early reading intervention, and Accelerated Reader® programs for use in shared, guided, and independent reading and writing activities to support a balanced approach to literacy instruction. The SandCastle™ series has four levels that correspond to early literacy development. The levels are provided to help teachers and parents select appropriate books for young readers.

Emerging Readers
(no flags)

Beginning Readers
(1 flag)

Transitional Readers
(2 flags)

Fluent Readers
(3 flags)

SandCastle™ would like to hear from you. Please send us your comments and suggestions.
sandcastle@abdopublishing.com

Vital Statistics

for the Beaver

BABY NAME
kit

NUMBER IN LITTER
1 to 4, average 3 to 4

WEIGHT AT BIRTH
1 pound

AGE OF INDEPENDENCE
2 years

ADULT WEIGHT
30 to 70 pounds

LIFE EXPECTANCY
10 to 12 years

A baby beaver is called a kit. There are no special names for mother and father beavers.

Beavers stay with one mate for life. They have a litter of one to four kits each year. Both parents share the duties of raising the kits.

Beavers are herbivores. They eat the small branches of trees such as aspen and birch. They also eat aquatic plants such as water lilies.

An herbivore is an animal that eats mostly plants.

Beavers build dams across rivers to create ponds. Then they build domed lodges in the ponds for their families to live in.

The sound of running water triggers a beaver's dam-building instinct.

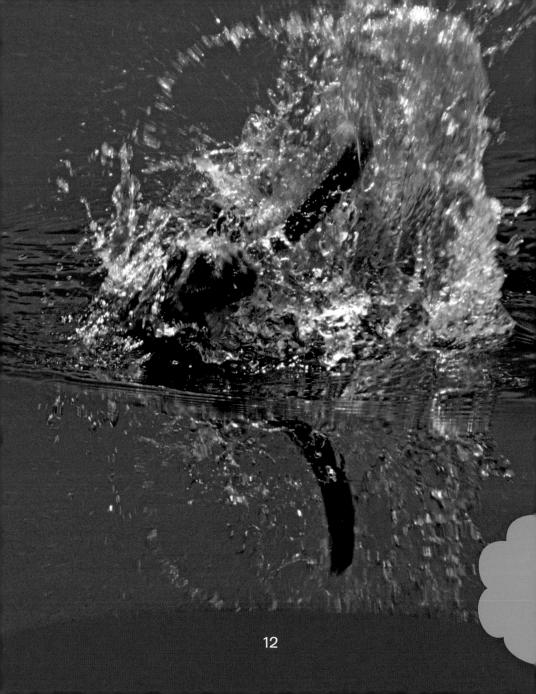

Beavers groan and hiss to communicate with each other. A beaver warns other beavers of danger by slapping its tail on the water.

A beaver kit can swim within 24 hours of being born. But if danger is near, the parents quickly carry the kits up into the lodge through an underwater entrance.

Wolves, coyotes, and lynx prey on beaver kits. However, humans cause the most harm to beavers through hunting, trapping, and accidental killing.

Beaver kits work with their parents. They help repair the lodge and the dam.

Beavers are able to stay underwater for up to 15 minutes.

When beaver kits are one year old, they help care for their newborn siblings. Kits stay with their families until they are about two years old.

Fun Fact

About the Beaver

In prehistoric times, the beaver was about eight feet long and weighed 500 pounds. That's bigger than a black bear! Although the modern beaver is much smaller, it is still the second-largest rodent in the world.

Glossary

accidental – not planned, often with harmful or damaging results.

communicate – to share ideas, information, or feelings.

dam – a barrier built to hold back water.

duty – a chore or task that must be done.

expectancy – an expected or likely amount.

herbivore – an animal that eats mainly plants.

independence – the state of no longer needing others to care for or support you.

instinct – a natural pattern of behavior that a species is born with.

lodge – a den where certain social animals, such as beavers, hide and live.

prey – to hunt or catch an animal for food.

To see a complete list of SandCastle™ books and other nonfiction titles from ABDO Publishing Company, visit **www.abdopublishing.com**.

8000 West 78th Street, Edina, MN 55439

800-800-1312 • 952-831-1632 fax